Road Maps and GPS

BY SAMANTHA S. BELL

The Child's World®
childsworld.com

Published by The Child's World®
1980 Lookout Drive • Mankato, MN 56003-1705
800-599-READ • www.childsworld.com

Photographs ©: Shutterstock Images, cover
(background), 1, 5; Vadim Georgiev/Shutterstock
Images, cover (foreground); Andrey Popov/
Shutterstock Images, 6; Dean Mitchell/iStockphoto,
9; Katherine Welles/Shutterstock Images, 10,
Sander van der Werf/Shutterstock Images, 15;
Alexander Lukatskiy/Shutterstock Images, 13;
iStockphoto, 16; Yin Yang/iStockphoto, 19

ISBN Hardcover: 9781503827752
ISBN Paperback: 9781622434534
LCCN: 2018944824

Printed in the United States of America
PA02397

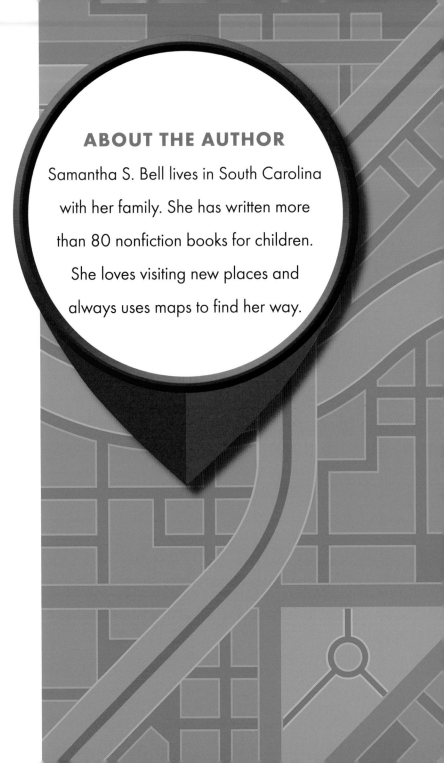

ABOUT THE AUTHOR

Samantha S. Bell lives in South Carolina with her family. She has written more than 80 nonfiction books for children. She loves visiting new places and always uses maps to find her way.

TABLE OF CONTENTS

CHAPTER ONE

Showing the Way

You and your family are planning a trip. First you need to decide where to go. Then you have to choose which **route** to take. You look at a road map to plan your trip.

Road maps show the streets or highways in a certain area. Some road maps are printed on paper. Others are **digital**. Drivers can see digital maps on computers or another electronic **device**.

Road maps
show which roads
to drive on.

A GPS can be on a smartphone or its own system.

Sometimes people do not use maps. They use a Global Positioning System (GPS) instead. A GPS is a digital system that shows people exactly where they are. It tells them how to get to a new location. It can also tell them how long it will take to get there.

Road maps and GPS are important tools for travelers. They help people get from one place to another without getting lost.

CHAPTER TWO

Road Maps

Most people use road maps when they go somewhere new. They help you prepare for the journey. The roads are drawn as lines on the map.

Some roads are small. They go through a city. Other roads are larger. They may go from one state to another. Wider lines **represent** bigger roads.

Road maps can be used on bike rides.

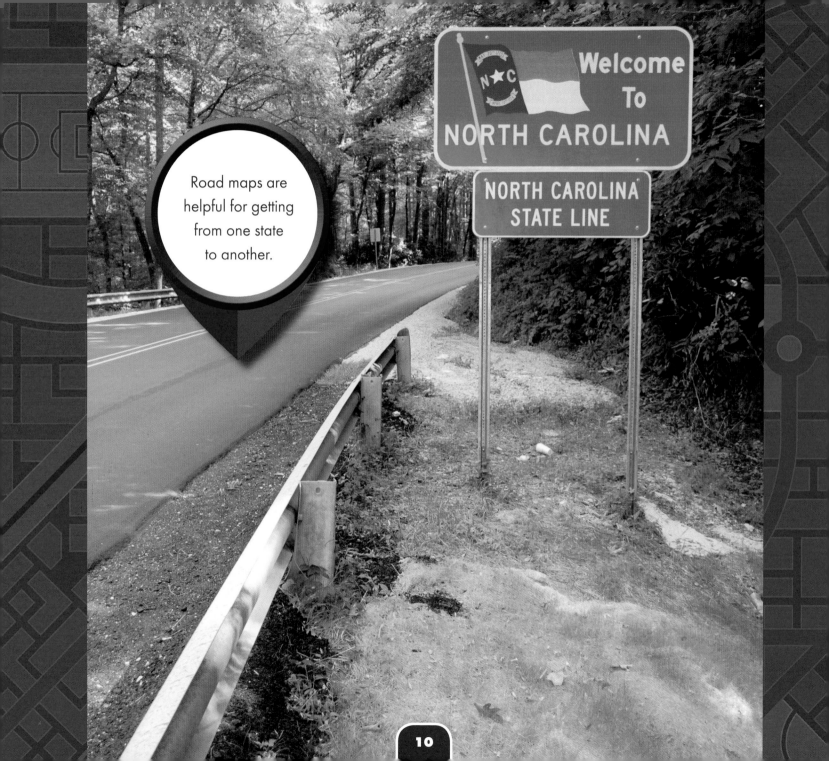

Road maps are helpful for getting from one state to another.

Welcome To
NORTH CAROLINA

NORTH CAROLINA STATE LINE

Many road maps show the **boundaries** between states. They show the location of cities and towns. They show natural features such as mountains and rivers.

Road maps provide other information travelers may need. Some tell the distance between cities. Some show speed limits for certain roads. They may show the location of hospitals and airports. Some show parks and other places people may want to visit.

Some road maps are on single sheets of paper. They are easy to fold and carry. Others are part of a road **atlas**. This type of book has many pages of maps.

Some people use computerized road maps. They can zoom out to see a large area such as a city or state. They can zoom in to see all the streets in a neighborhood.

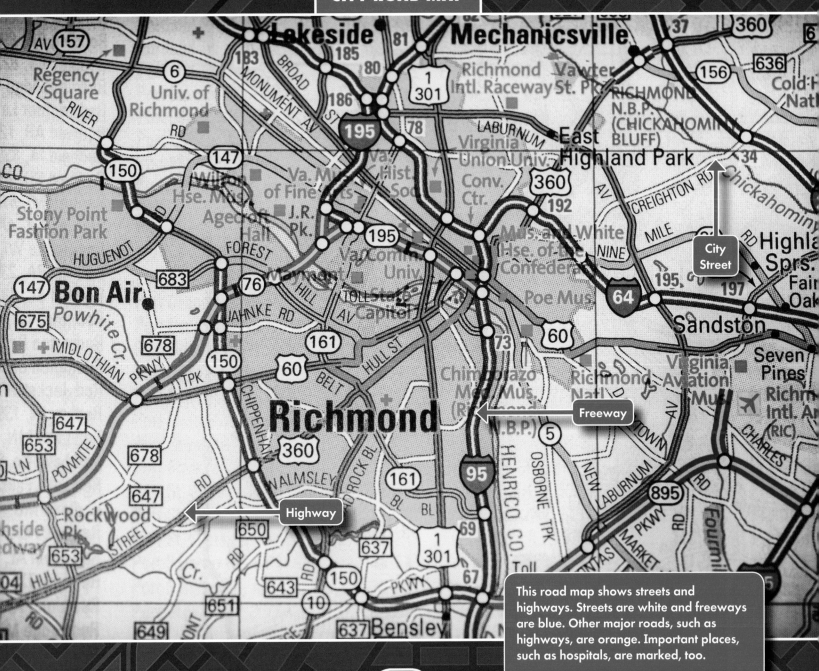

This road map shows streets and highways. Streets are white and freeways are blue. Other major roads, such as highways, are orange. Important places, such as hospitals, are marked, too.

CHAPTER THREE

GPS

Many people use GPS when they travel. It is made up of three parts. These include **satellites**, ground stations, and **receivers**.

The satellites are in space. They move around Earth. The ground stations keep track of the satellites. They make sure the satellites are working properly.

A GPS can be used for long hikes. It shows hikers where to go when there are no signs or roads.

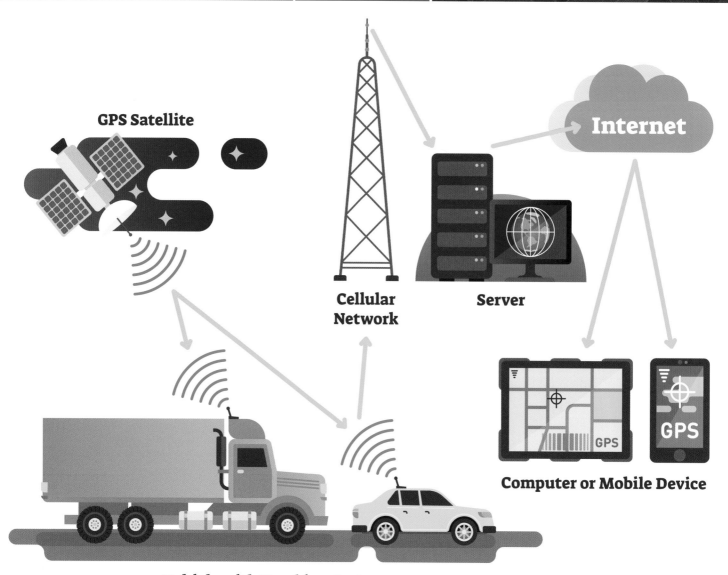

GPS Satellite

Cellular
Network

Server

Internet

Computer or Mobile Device

Vehicle with Tracking System

This shows how a GPS signal goes
from the satellite to the GPS device.

Each satellite sends down a **signal**. Receivers can pick up some of the signals. The receiver may be in a car or a phone. It must pick up at least four signals to work. The receiver figures out how far it is from the satellites. Then it can show the exact location on Earth.

Many people use GPS. Delivery drivers use it to find stores or businesses. Travelers use it when they go on vacation. Emergency workers use it to find people in trouble.

Road maps and GPS help people find their way. They provide them with information about their destinations.

Pizza drivers use GPS to help find the locations of their deliveries.

19

Do You Know?

Q: What do the lines represent on a road map?

A: Highways and city streets

Q: Where are GPS satellites found?

A: Space

Q: When would you use a road map?

Q: What kind of information can be found on a road map?

Glossary

atlas (AT-luhss) An atlas is a book of maps. Some people use an atlas when they go on vacation.

boundaries (BOWN-duh-reez) Boundaries are dividing lines that show the end or limit of something. Some maps show the boundaries between states.

device (di-VYSS) A device is something made for a purpose, such as a piece of mechanical or electronic equipment. A cell phone is a device that can receive GPS signals.

digital (DIJ-uh-tuhl) Digital refers to something that uses electronic or computer technology. Some people use digital maps on their cell phones.

receivers (ri-SEE-vurz) Receivers are pieces of technology that get GPS signals. Receivers need at least four satellite signals to find your location.

represent (rep-ri-ZENT) To represent means to serve as a sign for something else. Lines on a map can represent roads.

route (ROWT) A route is the way you follow to get from one place to another. Travelers follow the fastest route.

satellites (SAT-uh-lites) Satellites are man-made objects that travel around the earth, the moon, or another object in space. Satellites look like stars moving across the sky.

signal (SIG-nuhl) A signal is a radio wave or electric current that carries information. A GPS can use a signal from a satellite in space.

To Learn More

BOOKS

National Geographic Kids United States Atlas.
Washington, DC: National Geographic, 2017.

Olien, Rebecca. *Looking at Maps and Globes*.
New York, NY: Children's Press, 2013.

Quinlan, Julia J. *GPS and Computer Maps*.
New York, NY: Powerkids Press, 2012.

WEB SITES

Visit our Web site for links about road maps and GPS:
childsworld.com/links

Note to Parents, Teachers, and Librarians: We routinely verify our Web Links to make sure they are safe and active sites. So encourage your readers to check them out!

Index